Opening up Values
Learning from religion

Values development is at the heart school life – it is central to the development of children, helping them to lead fulfilling lives, be happy and confident, responsible and willing to make a positive contribution to society.

Many schools take a whole school approach to values development and RE has a key role to play in this. Values are the principles or convictions that act as a guide to our behaviour. They are concerned with beliefs about what is of fundamental worth, and these beliefs impact on actions. This is at the heart of religious education.

RE activities can underpin whole school approaches by helping children to make the link between what we believe and how we behave. Many values originate in the wisdom of the faith traditions and in the teaching of key religious figures. Reflective exploration of these provides a great opportunity for the spiritual and moral development of children at the same time as doing great RE, helping them learn about and learn from religion. A key outcome is that children should be able to consider their own beliefs and values and those of others in the light of their learning in religious education.

The wisdom of the faith traditions and teachings of key religious figures provide a wonderful resource for helping children explore and reflect upon values such as love, peace, unity and service. This publication suggests stories, activities and other materials from six world faiths linked to seven of these key spiritual values.

Joyce Mackley

Editor

Contents

LEARNING FROM CHRISTIAN VALUES: LOVE

For the teacher

- Love is the central concept in Christianity. Jesus summed up his teachings by giving his followers the Two Great Commandments: to love God and to love your neighbour as yourself. (Luke 10: 27)

- To explain this further, Jesus told the parable of the Good Samaritan. This teaches that love is unselfish giving for the benefit of others.

- This kind of love does not depend on feelings, or affection, or attraction, but is a commitment to look for the best in others and does not change whether the love given is returned or not.

The activities suggested here aim to:

- help younger children to reflect on love in their own lives, recall a story from Jesus and think about how we show love to others, whilst engaging in creative and expressive activities on the theme of love.

- help older primary children to consider the importance of love in the foundations for their own lives and to get to the heart of Christian teaching about love through engaging with a Bible 'love poem', a well-known prayer and a story from today.

What can children do as a result of this unit?

The following pupil-friendly 'I can . . .' statements describe the learning that may be expected of pupils.

Level   Description of achievement: I can . . .

1
- **recall a story** Jesus told about loving others.
- **talk about** people who love me and whom I love, and how I show this love.

2
- **retell a story** Jesus told about loving others and talk about what can be learnt from it.
- **choose or make a symbol** and decorate it to show what 'love your neighbour' means to me.

3
- **describe** some ways in which Christians put the teaching of Jesus on love into action.
- **make links** between Christian ideas about love and my own ideas (AT2).

4
- **show that I understand** Christian ideas about love and can **describe** some ways people today put this type of love into action.
- come up with some **questions** I would ask a Christian about following Jesus' teaching on love and **suggest** what **answers** they might give.
- **express thoughtfully and creatively** my own ideas about love in light of my learning about Christian ideas.

'I give you a new commandment, that you love one another. As I have loved you, you should also love one another.'

Bible: John ch 13 v 34

'You show love for others by truly helping them, and not by merely talking about it.'

Bible: 1 John ch 3 v 18

Cross-curricular links

Literacy: speaking; listening and responding; group discussion and interaction; drama (role play); understanding and interpreting texts; engaging with and responding to texts; creating and shaping texts

Creativity – through Art and DT activities

PSHCE – working with others, discussing beliefs, values and practices, collaborating with others and developing respect and sensitivity.

RE Today
Services

Activities from the classroom: 'Love' - a cross-curricular theme for 4–5 year olds

Class 1 at Stoke Prior Community Primary School, Herefordshire, enjoyed an RE-led theme which used skills from literacy, art, DT and PSHCE.

The theme enabled children to:

- **listen to, and talk about,** a secular story and a story from the Bible about loving others (The Good Samaritan)

- **have times of quiet and stillness for reflection.** Following the circle time story, children took a heart shape from a circular cloth (with lighted candle) as they spoke about people they loved and who loved them.

- **make and do** – transforming the role-play corner into a church by adding a clock tower, a lectern, crosses, a chalice and a plate (made from card covered in foil), flowers and an altar; making symbols of love to decorate it for a wedding; dressing up and role-playing a Christian wedding; making (and eating!) heart-shaped biscuits; making a stained glass window for the 'church' to show the story of the Good Samaritan.

- **begin to use ICT to explore religious beliefs:** children used digital cameras to record the Christian wedding which took place in the role-play church.

They had great fun. The carefully planned activities encouraged children to use their imagination and curiosity, to share their own beliefs, ideas and values, and to talk about their feelings and experiences whilst developing knowledge and understanding of the Christian value of love. All are essential elements of great RE learning – and central to the Early Years curriculum.

The activities enabled children to achieve the following outcomes expected by the local Agreed Syllabus for RE:

- **talk about** people who love them and whom they love and how they show this love

- **recall stories** Jesus told about loving others and talk about what can be learnt from them

- **begin to understand** that the church is a special place for Christians.

A key tip for planning cross curricular RE:

Make sure it is RE! Are the activities planned around the expected outcomes set out in your local agreed syllabus or faith community guidelines (in the case of Aided schools)?

Christian lives are rooted in Jesus. In what are our lives rooted?

This activity uses the metaphor of the tree and its fruits to help children reflect on the qualities and virtues that make a good person.

Classroom activities

- Look at a plant. Lift it out of the pot and examine its root system. Talk about: Why does the plant need roots? What would happen if the roots were chopped off?

- In what ways are we like this plant? We might not have 'roots' that we can see – but we all need lots of good things to help us live and 'produce' good things in our lives. We can all see wonderful red shiny apples on a tree – what wonderful things do we want people to see in our lives?

- Give children in pairs two copies of the tree diagram (downloadable from the RE Today website)

  - On one, write down what a tree needs from its roots to help it grow big and strong – water, minerals, nutrients from the ground, and so on. Encourage children to create some wonderful new fruits that this tree produces.

  - On the other, think about the good things we need if we are to grow and flourish as people. Start off by making the **fruits**. What are the wonderful qualities we find in great people and in those who love us? Make some wonderful fruits for the tree and write these qualities and virtues on them.

  - **Roots:** Ask children to consider the foundations for their lives (e.g. friends and family, activities that strengthen them, spiritual foundations) and what would happen if these changed or went away?

  - Use appropriate activities to help children reflecton the important values which help us grow into good people, e.g. truthfulness, kindness, tolerance and so on. Children can record these in a visual way by writing them in on the roots of their tree.

- **Love** – this is one quality that is likely to appear on everyone's tree. Jesus taught his followers to 'Love God and to love your neighbour as you love yourself'. Ask children to suggest what this means and how Christians might put this into practice today. If children agree that loving others is the most important value, they could write the word LOVE on the trunk of their trees.

This outline, together with a pupil activity can be downloaded from the RE Today website www.retoday.org.uk

Prayer of St Francis of Assisi

Jesus,

help me to bring your peace to everyone. . .

To bring love where there is hate. . .

To forgive people who have been unkind. . .

To bring together people who are arguing. . .

To tell the truth when others tell lies. . .

To believe in you when others do not. . .

To be hopefull when others give up. . .

To bring light wherever there is darkness. . .

To bring happiness wherever there is sadness. . .

Jesus,

I will comfort others,

I will love others,

I will understand others.

I'm making others happy,

I will become closer to you

and happier in myself.

Amen.

Prayer of ....

Help me to . . .

....

....

....

....

....

....

....

....

....

I will . . .

....

....

....

....

....

Give children a copy of this prayer or display it on the interactive whiteboard.

Using this child-friendly version of the famous traditional Christian prayer of St Francis of Assisi:

Ask children (in pairs) to:

- Find at least five contrast statements (e.g. love hate)
- Identify and highlight Christian values (some they might find are: peace, love, forgiveness, truthfulness, faith –'to believe in you' – hope)
- compare their findings with others.

Help children notice the structure of the prayer:

The first part is *asking*

'help me to . . .'

followed by nine statements: e.g.

'to bring peace to everyone

'to bring love where there is hate' etc.

Here St Francis sets out his hopes and dreams for a better, happier world. Christians would say he is describing the sort of world God wants for everyone.

In the second part St Francis is 'promising' or 'committing himself' to take action to help to bring this kinder, better world about

'I will . . .'

Ask children to use the writing scaffold to help them write their own version of the prayer or, if more appropriate, to write it as a reflection rather than a prayer by changing *'Help me . . .'* into *'I hope for a world in which . . .'*

Cross-curricular links

RE

Literacy

Personal Development

Skills

- **Reflection**
- **Analysis**
- **Interpretation**
- **Expression**
- **Use of appropriate vocabulary**

I Corinthians 13: a love 'poem' from St Paul

1 What if I could speak all languages of humans and of angels? **If I did not love others, I would be nothing more than a noisy gong or a clanging cymbal.**

2 What if I could prophesy and understand all secrets and all knowledge? And what if I had faith that moved mountains? **I would be nothing, unless I loved others.**

3 What if I gave away all that I owned and let myself be burned alive? **I would gain nothing, unless I loved others.**

4 Love is kind and patient, never jealous, boastful, proud, or 5rude.

Love isn't selfish or quick tempered. It doesn't keep a record of wrongs that others do.

6 Love rejoices in the truth, but not in evil.

7 Love is always supportive, loyal, hopeful and trusting.

8 Love never fails!

12 Now all we can see of God is like a cloudy picture in a mirror.

Later we will see him face to face.

We don't know everything, but then we will, just as God completely understands us.

13 For now there are faith, hope, and love.

But of these three, the greatest is love.

Classroom activities

- Ask four good readers to read this aloud, with each person reading one of the colour-coded sections.*

- Encourage this small group to practise this and to perform it with a real sense of occasion.

- Tell pupils it is the most famous 2000-year-old love poem in the world, and defines Christian love.

- When they've heard it, ask all the children – in pairs – to create their own using the framework on this page.

- What would the world be like if people put this sort of love into action? Pupils could use their creativity to show this in a variety of ways (e.g. dance, artwork, drama)

Love is . . .
Love is . . .
Love is . . .

What if . . .
What if . . .
What if . . .

I gain nothing unless . . .
I gain nothing unless . . .
I gain nothing unless . . .

Love is not . . .
Love is not . . .
Love is not . . .

Love is always . . .
Love is always . . .
Love is always . . .

* Subscribers may download a copy of this poem from the RE Today website: www.retoday.org.uk

RE Today
Services

A story about love in action today

'My best Christmas ever' by Paul Owen

I've always enjoyed a family Christmas with loads of laughs and presents. We throw parties, and go to parties. But my best Christmas ever was when I was 23. That year, I'd just finished college, and I decided to volunteer to work for the Cyrenians. It's a charity that helps homeless people. They sent me to work in Bristol, and I was part of a great team. Four of us worked at a day centre for homeless people in the big upstairs room of a Methodist church. We also did a 'soup run'. We would go all round the city centre and take hot soup in the middle of the night to people who slept in doorways or derelict buildings.

I learned that homeless people aren't bad people – they have been unlucky in life. Many of them are talented, able, skilful and kind in their own way.

For Christmas, we decided to keep the day centre open for four days, from Christmas Eve to the day after Boxing Day. We asked lots of local schools to help raise funds. Many did so, to sponsor a meal for our 65 homeless people. We begged and borrowed some decorations. A bunch of the homeless people who were musical got together. They stood round a piano and sang loads of Christmas songs. It wasn't 'Silent Night', but it warmed your heart. Outside it was freezing.

Usually at our day centre there could be a fight or an argument, and Christmas was like that too, but at the same time we all felt a kind of warm spirit.

Volunteers came in for a few hours to wash up, cook or help out – or, best of all, just to sit and chat, and make the party atmosphere work a bit. It was friendly. People talked about their childhood, and what Christmas had been like for them long ago.

It was exhausting – very busy and with not a moment to think. But when the day centre closed at the end of the four days, and I sat down to think, I realised three ways this was my best Christmas.

First, Jesus was born homeless – laid in a manger, born in a barn. Spending Christmas with homeless people reminded me of what it was really all about.

Second, I'm a Christian, and Jesus wants his followers to try and love others, especially those in need. Christmas with Cyrenians taught me how to do this.

Third, Christmas in the shops often feels as if it's all about how rich you are, and how much you spend. But my homeless friends showed me that good celebrations don't depend on spending money.

Activities for pupils

Questions to think and talk about:

Where in the story do the following ideas from the Bible show through?

Patient

Kind

Supportive

Loyal

Hopeful

Trusting

How are these seen in Paul's Christmas story?

Find out more about Simon of Cyrene (Mark ch 15 vs 20-22) and the work of the Cyrenians today in your local area.

Would the following quotation make a good 'motto' for their work? Explain your ideas.

'You show love for others by truly helping them, and not by merely talking about it.'

Bible: John ch 13 v 14

LEARNING FROM JEWISH VALUES: HOPE

For the teacher

Religions give their followers a vision, or a hope for the future, for humanity, for the world and beyond.

Religions find outward ways of expressing this inner hope. This is often through story, symbol and festivals.

The following suggested activities focus on helping children reflect on the value of hope, using story, symbols and a festival from Judaism.

- **story:** Noah and the rainbow; the hope that faith gives
- **symbols:** rainbow, Hanukkiah
- **festival:** Hanukkah.

Information file

- Versions of the Noah story are found in the scriptures of three religions: *Judaism, Christianity* and *Islam*.

- Festivals are often outward ways of expressing inner hopes. The main theme of the Jewish festival of Hanukkah is the promise of God's faithfulness, which gives hope and confidence in times of darkness.

- Jews made a bargain (covenant) with God to keep his laws. Being part of a community that follows particular customs and rules binds people together and gives them a sense of identity.

Cross-curricular links

- 'RE in the curriculum', a short film showing aspects of the cross-curricular activities described on page 12 can be downloaded from www.natre.org.uk

- The song 'When You Believe' (Prince of Egypt) used in the presentation on page 11 can be downloaded from www.homeofhope.co.uk and the lyrics from http://homeofhope.co.uk/Documents/HomeofHope.pdf

What can children do as a result of this unit?

The following pupil-friendly 'I can . . .' statements describe the learning that may be expected of pupils.

Level Description of achievement: I can . . .

1
- **recognise** a rainbow and talk about a story from the Bible it reminds me of.
- **talk about** something Noah might have hoped for when he came out of the ark and something I hope for.

2
- **pick out** two key moments in the story of Noah, and **suggest meanings** for the rainbow and the dove.
- make a good symbol to represent hope and write about something I hope for.

3
- **make a link** between the Jewish story of Hanukkah or Noah and the value of hope, and say how the story might help someone today.
- thoughtfully complete the rainbow grid **making a link** between the Noah story and our class's hopes.

4
- **ask some thoughtful 'Why?' questions** linked to the Jewish stories and **suggest some answers** Jewish people might give.
- **describe** my own ideas about hope in a poem, a painting or a design, applying these ideas to myself and life today.

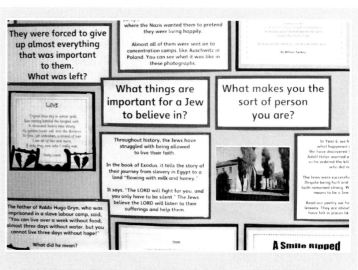

A Year 6 wall display: St Pauls's CE Primary School, Hereford

A story about hope: Noah and the rainbow

For the teacher

- This activity aims to enable children to consider the idea of 'hope' from the story of Noah and the rainbow, and to use it to clarify and stimulate their own hopes.

- When using the biblical Noah story, avoid 'watering' it down to merely a story about animals or water. It has deep theological significance for people of three world faiths. For younger children a focus on promises and hopes is appropriate. For older children the key themes of judgement and salvation may appropriately be explored.

Classroom activities

- Retell the story of Noah well using an authentic children's Bible version. The original story is in Genesis Chapters 6–9.

Talk about

- the symbols of hope in the story – leaf, dove, rainbow.

- what do we mean by hope?

- children's examples of things they hope for.

Choose one of the following creative expressive activities

- Give children a raindrop shape. Write or draw on this 'threats, dangers or fears'. Give them a leaf shape. On this ask them to draw their 'hopes'

- Ask them to make a work of art to show **'a moment of hope'** from the story.

- The rainbow is often used as a symbol of hope. What did it mean to Noah? What does it mean to you?

- Use the rainbow and the grid from page 9 to structure children's own reflective thinking on the theme of hope. Children could talk through ideas together, but then complete the grids individually.

The story of Noah and the rainbow

God was very angry. When he looked at the beautiful world he had made, he saw the bad things people were doing to it and to each other. It made him very sad.

He decided the world needed a fresh start!

He had noticed one good man and his family and he decided that he would ask him to help. The man was called Noah.

God told Noah to build a boat. A boat big enough to take his family, and two each of all the different animals and birds in the world. What an enormous boat it must have been!

No sooner had Noah finished building this enormous boat, and gathering in all the different birds and animals, than the rain started. It poured and poured – day and night. The floods rose until no land could be seen. A great sea spread over the whole world.

The boat floated for days and weeks and months . . . until one day it stopped. It had found some land at last. The flood was beginning to go down.

Noah sent out a dove carrying their hopes for a fresh new earth! When she returned with an olive leaf, Noah felt hope rise in his heart. He sent her out again. This time she didn't return. He knew that at last she had found a new home and he thanked God.

In the clear blue sky a beautiful rainbow shone. Seven stripes of liquid light poured down. Noah saw this as a sign that never again would God destroy the earth. Noah's heart was filled with joy and thankfulness.

Expressing hope

	Noah's hopes Write into this column some of the things you think Noah hoped for	Our class's hopes Write into this column some of the things your class hopes for
Red: A hope for myself		
Orange: A hope for my family		
Yellow: A hope for the animals		
Green: A hope for the future		
Blue: A hope for fairness		
Indigo: A hope for friendship		
Purple: A hope for the whole world		

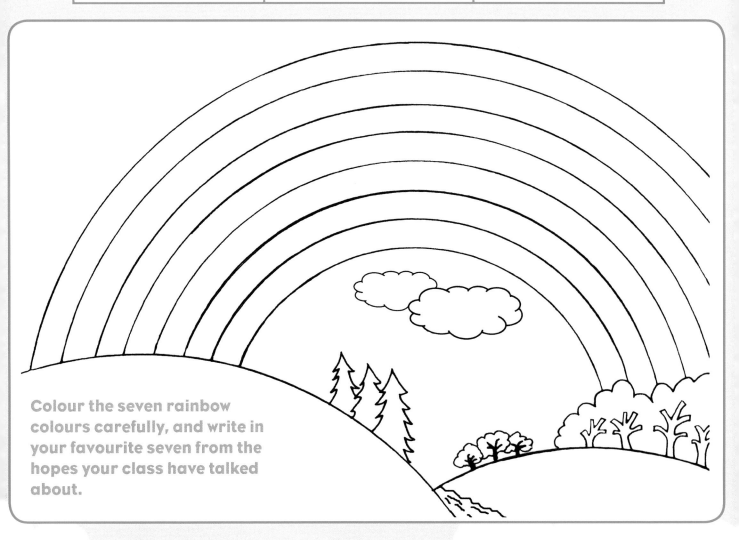

Colour the seven rainbow colours carefully, and write in your favourite seven from the hopes your class have talked about.

RE Today Services

Jewish story: Hanukkah in the concentration camps

The story behind the Jewish festival of Hanukkah: an exploring and expressing activity

- Using a children's version, tell the story of Judah 'the Macabbee' (the story commemorated at the Jewish festival of Hanukkah). Light a 9-branched candlestick or Hanukkiah at the appropriate point in the story (a downloadable version of the story is available for subscribers from the RE Today website). Talk about why it has nine branches.

- Explain how Hanukkah is celebrated every year. It is a happy time which gives people hope for the future.

- Talk about pupils' own hopes – remind them of the wishes they make for themselves when they blow out birthday candles. Produce Hanukkiah cut-outs stuck on large sheets of sugar paper. Using the writing frame below, pupils reflect on their own hopes for the future and write these on flame-shaped cut-outs. These are stuck on the paper Hanukkiah and displayed around the room.

Talk about

- What did Hugo's dad mean?
- Do you agree with him?
- What gives you hope for the future?
- How can faith in God give people hope?

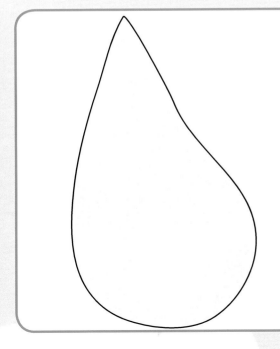

Hanukkah Hopes

My hope for myself.........................

My hope for my family.........................

My hope for my school ....

Activities from the classroom

As part of a cross-curricular unit on the Second World War, Year 6 children at St Paul's CE Primary School, Hereford, explored the questions of 'What does it mean to be Jewish?' and 'Do religious beliefs help people survive in times of suffering?'

Here children describe what they did:

In RE we

- read what a Jewish boy called Samuel believed was important in his life today, what his special times were and what he might change about his life. We thought about and made comparisons with our own lives too.
- did some role-play about the events on the Exodus to show how God would care for the Hebrew people in times of trouble.
- had small group and class discussions about Jews and their experiences of the Holocaust. We talked about the ways they tried to continue their traditions such as trying to use margarine rations to light the menorah in the labour camp. This was Rabbi Hugo Gryn's story.
- imagined what it must be like to be persecuted, and thought how strong the Jews must have been to cope with the torture.

In History we discovered how and why the war began. We learnt about evacuation and how children experienced going away from home. We learnt about the Blitz, what happened and how people tried to keep safe from the bombing raids.

In Literacy we

- read poetry from the young people who were held in the Terezin ghetto.
- noticed they used metaphors and imagery with powerful vocabulary to create a picture of their feelings. We tried to think about how abstract nouns, such as happiness, despair, hope and fear, might look as a metaphor, and used poetry techniques such as similes, kennings and alliteration to produce our own poems on the theme of 'Hope'.

RE Today would love to share these with others in future publications.

Contact the Primary Curriculum series editor at RE Today.

View a short film of this activity. See details on page 8

A presentation: an extract from a presentation to parents prepared by the Year 6 children

Narrator: In a labour camp, the father of a modern Jewish leader, Rabbi Hugo Gryn, taught his son an important lesson. Let's hear the story.

Hugo: Dad, it's Hanukkah soon, we have to celebrate it. Doesn't it commemorate the time the Israelites ran out of oil for the lamp in the temple? They prayed to God and it was a miracle. The oil lasted for eight days. Amazing eh?

Dad: That's right, Hugo. Even though we're in this hole of a place, we'll remember that time. Look, you're in charge of making a wick for the candle.

Hugo: And so I take an old guard's cap and pull the threads and twist them to make the wick. What do we do for the candle?

Dad: Even though we have the worst food possible, all of us will save our tiny margarine rations over the next few days. We'll put it into an old container and wait for Hanukkah to come.

Jew I: Have this margarine – don't let the guards see you with it. Hide it quick. It's sunset and we're ready. Let's be still.

Hugo: I'm the youngest here.

Dad: So you're in charge of lighting. There's a match.

Hugo: I light the match. My heart is beating so loudly. There is quiet in the hut. I bring the flame to the wick but it doesn't stay alight. Nothing. All that work for nothing. And we can't rejoice with God. I'm not upset, I'm angry! You stupid fools, do you not know that margarine won't burn!

Dad: Sit here and listen, Hugo. We went without food for a week. We cannot survive without water for three days. But we would not survive three minutes without hope.

Narrator: Isn't hope important? Without hope our lives would be dark. For Christians, they believe that Jesus is their true hope, a light that shines in the darkness. For Jews, for Christians, for Muslims, for those of no belief, hope is about looking forward to the future. Believing in yourself is part of it. If you believe, then what you hope for will happen.

Dance Pupils perform a dance on the theme of 'hope' to the song 'When You Believe' (*Prince of Egypt*). See Information File on page 9 for details.

LEARNING FROM MUSLIM VALUES: PEACE

For the teacher

- Peace is a central concept in Islam. 'Islam' means 'peace' – it is usually described as the peace gained through willing submission to Allah. A Muslim is 'one who submits to Allah' in this way. Willing submission brings peace.

- Peace is a universal value, although we do not always see it practised.

- Children can consider the meaning of peace in Islam as a way into thinking about the importance of peace in their own lives, and the possibility of sharing it with others.

- The activities suggested here aim to help children to begin to realise that inner beliefs and feelings can be expressed outwardly – and to help them to begin to explore the meaning of images and actions.

How to use this unit

The focus in this unit is to understand peace in Islam. For it to be good RE, it is essential to ensure that the 'exploring peace' activities are used as a way into exploring 'peace' in the context of Islam. Avoid falling into the trap of stopping after the child-focused values activities!

The activities on pages 14–16 are planned as a complete unit, working with 5–7 year olds – taking an afternoon session, perhaps. The steps are:

1 **engaging** children with peace in Islam by looking at various greetings.

2 **exploring** what we mean by peace.

3 **expressing** what children think and feel about peace in themselves.

4 **applying** these ideas to peace in Islam.

5 allowing children to **reflect** on and **respond** to what they have learned.

Pages 17–18 address the idea of peace as willing submission – this is for 7–11 year olds.

What can children do as a result of this unit?

The following pupil-friendly 'I can . . .' statements describe the learning that may be expected of pupils.

Level	Description of achievement: I can . . .
1	• **recognise** how Muslims say hello to each other and what this means. • **talk about** how peace matters to me.
2	• **say why** peace is important to Muslims. • **recognise** why peace is important to me and to others.
3	• **identify** what brings peace to Muslims and how they behave because of this. • **show how** my ideas about peace affect how I behave.
4	• **show that I understand** how submitting to Allah can bring peace to a Muslim. • come up with some **questions** I would ask a Muslim about submission, and **suggest** what **answers** they might give. • **compare** this to how I find peace and others find peace.

Activity 1   What do people mean when they say hello?

- Ask the children if they can pick out the letters that are found in all three of the following words:

ISLAM   MUSLIM   SALAAM

They should identify the letters **S L M**.

In Arabic, this word, *slm*, means **peace**.

Explain that when Muslims greet each other, they say **As-salaam alaikum** (*a*-**lay-kum**). It means 'Peace be with you'. In reply, a Muslim will say, **'Wa-alaikum as-salaam'** – which means 'And peace be with you too.'

- Give children some of the words people use to greet each other in other languages.

- Get the children to walk around, practising the words as they greet each other. They could each hold a symbol and a picture of a child representing one of the religions – as they meet someone they need to try and recognise the symbol and say the correct greeting. (Either copy the images on the right or download from the RE Today website, if you are a subscriber.)

- Gather together to talk about what difference it might make if everyone said 'Peace be with you' instead of 'Hello', whenever they greet each other.

- Explain that the Prophet Muhammad ﷺ told Muslims to greet each other in this way – 'Peace be with you'. Muslims are asking God to send peace to the person they greet. Talk about why this is lovely thing to do.

Grace   Arjan

Tanya   Samit

Activity 2   Exploring – What are you full of?

Getting started: Ask a child to act out carrying a cup full of water.

Talk about: What will happen if someone bumps into the child carrying the water? What is spilled out of the cup?

Think about: What are the children full of? What happens when they are 'bumped' during the day?

Talk about: What sorts of feelings and emotions do we hold inside us? – e.g. happy; sad; cross. How do we know that someone is feeling these? – e.g. smiling and laughing; crying; frowning or shouting.

Ask them to imagine that **they** are full of **peace** – what would happen if someone bumped into them? What would they do or say?

Imran   Hannah

Information file

Shalom – Hebrew for 'peace'; a Jewish greeting – it can be used for 'Hello' and 'Goodbye'. Jews sometimes say **'Shalom Aleichem'** – 'peace be with you'. You can see that this is very similar to the Muslim greeting.

Namaste (*namas-tay*) – A Hindu greeting meaning 'I bow to you'. This is usually accompanied by a slight bow, with hands pressed together, fingertips pointed upwards, held close to the chest.

'Goodbye' is a shortened form of 'God be with you' – a Christian term of blessing as you leave someone. (Most people don't use it like that today.)

RE Today
Services

Activity 3   Are you full of peace – or 'peaceful'?

To help children **express** ideas about what they are full of, bring in a selection of fabrics and other materials. These should be a variety of textures, from smooth and soft through to rough and knotted.

- **Ask children to** choose a texture or colour that reflects the idea of being peaceful. Why have they chosen this?

- **Talk about** some other feelings – such as feeling happy, sad, angry, hopeful, excited, kind, worried, and so on. Readers in the class may like to choose some from a word bank of feelings (see below).

- Children should **choose fabrics** to represent several feelings that they have – a fabric for each different feeling.

- **Give them an outline of a child** (copy and enlarge the examples below, which are also available from the RE Today website). They should choose the fabrics that show the feelings they have inside them. Use lots of the fabric if they think they have lots of this feeling inside. Use a little, if they only have this feeling a little, or occasionally.

- Children should stick the fabrics/materials onto the outline to express themselves. As they do this, they can **talk about** what they are filled with and how this is shown in how they behave. Remind them about the cup full of water and what spills out. **Talk about** how inner feelings can be expressed outwardly. If you cannot find sufficiently diverse fabrics and materials, this activity could be done with colours to represent feelings, using coloured tissue paper.

Thea's peaceful outline

Feelings word bank

Brave
Friendly
Angry
Confused
Excited
Joyful
Happy
Keen
Miserable
Nervous
Tired
Worried
Guilty
Confident
Shy
Disgusted
Scared
Ashamed
Sorry
Hopeful
Lonely
Surprised
Bored
Determined

NB

Remember that the focus for this is about peace in Islam, so keep referring back to the greeting - 'Peace be with you'.

To make this an effective learning activity for RE, you should complete this unit with the tasks on p16!

Activity 4   Peace in Islam

Link back to the children's pictures in Activity 3 which reflected their feelings inside. Feelings can change – so if we are often angry, or upset, we can try and change.

Talk about: What could you do to fill up with peace? e.g. sit quietly; say sorry; smile; listen to music; laugh; talk with your friends.

W Show children the picture below (down-loadable by subscribers from the RE Today website).

Ask children: What do you think is happening here? How do you think these people feel? How do you know? Why are they feeling like this?

Prayer is one way a Muslim can fill up with peace. Muslims see peace as a gift they gain from doing what Allah says. Muslims believe that Allah tells them to pray – so praying brings peace.

Activity 5   Reflect and respond

Ask children: *If peace is a gift, how would you share it with others?*

• Children might suggest that they would help each other if they are stuck, or comfort them if they are upset, or use only kind words.

• One way is to greet each other with peace! Try repeating the 'greetings' activity from the start of this unit – greeting with peace in different languages.

• Ask them to come up with one action that they will try and do to bring peace in their family – ask them to try it at home tonight!

©David Rose and NATRE 2009

What do Muslims mean by submission to Allah? How does it give them peace?

7–11

What do Muslims mean by submission to Allah?
How does it give them peace?

Activity 1   Trust games

Purpose: to help children

- learn about the value of trust
- understand how for Muslims it is submission to the will of Allah – trusting that God knows best – that brings peace.

Try these trust games

- Blindfold a child and ask her to find her way (carefully!) across the classroom to one of her friends. The friend might move away very quietly to make it more difficult. How easy was it to find the friend?

- Blindfold another child. Ask him to find someone in the class. This time he can be given verbal instructions by another friend. How easy was it this time?

- Blindfold another child. This time she can be guided by someone without a blindfold, who takes her hand or arm to lead her. How easy was it this time? Why? How did she feel about her guide? Why did she let the guide lead her across the classroom?

Ask children to think of some other examples of where a person might willingly give way to a greater authority: e.g. when lost and someone knows the way; if they are about to take a free kick for their football team – and [footballer of choice!] offers to take it for the team; or . . .?

Activity 2

Display a photograph or a still from a video clip of Muslim prayer. In pairs ask pupils to talk about:

- What do you think this person is doing?
- How does this link with the previous activity – about willing submission?
- How does this action show submission? How else might a Muslim show submission to God? List at least three ways.

Introduce the following quotations. Ask pupils to respond to the questions:

- Why do Muslims pray?
- How does it make them feel?

©RE Today Services 2005

For a range of Muslim pupil responses, go to www.natre.org.uk 'Children Talking'. Select 'What others have said', fill in the search options and look at Q7 'prayer makes me feel…'

'As I have to pray many times during the day, I've found that it helps to put my mind away from work and on God. Islam brings peace to me as I feel that I know what I have been created to do, which is to worship God.'

Razwan

'Prayer makes me feel calm in some way. Before I pray I am tense and when I am finished I feel calm. Prayer is when you show God how much you respect and love him.'

Aisha, 14

'Prayer makes me feel happy. It makes me fear God but also it makes me feel closer to God.'

Rafiq, 12

Activity 3

Read what Nasima says about being a Muslim.

Around the picture below, write down the things that give her peace.

See if you can think of things that would **stop** Nasima having peace. Write them here:

Islam gives me comfort, support and peace in many ways. For example, when I hear the call to prayer, I know that Muslims all over the world are getting ready for the prayer – this helps me to do it too.

Islam brings peace in the calmness and stillness of the prayer movements. That is when your mind is free from all the busy things in life and nothing else matters apart from this moment to talk to Allah.

How do I feel when I pray? Before I pray, I may feel worried about my day and how busy it is. As I prepare, covering my hair and washing, I start to relax. The ritual helps me to calm down.

Once I have done my prayers, I feel like an invisible force is hugging me, I feel comforted and safe. I feel protected and warm. I feel as if I have recharged my energy levels, and can continue with my day.

Nasima Hassan

Draw your face in the middle of this box.

Around it, write down the things that give you peace. Some of them may be like Nasima's ideas – some of them may be different.

Think about what things **stop** you having peace.

Write some ideas here. (You don't have to write things that you find upsetting or difficult. You can keep those ideas to yourself.)

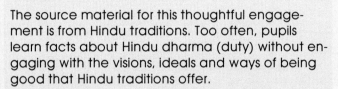

LEARNING FROM HINDU VALUES: BEING GOOD

For the teacher

These lesson ideas are designed to help your pupils to think for themselves about what is good and bad, nice and nasty, kind and unkind.

The source material for this thoughtful engagement is from Hindu traditions. Too often, pupils learn facts about Hindu dharma (duty) without engaging with the visions, ideals and ways of being good that Hindu traditions offer.

Among all the religions commonly taught in RE, 'Hinduism' is the most diverse. Teachers will be used to saying 'some Hindus . . .' or 'many Hindu people . . .' in all their work. The examples presented here show just small glimpses of the 'eternal way' (the Sanatan Dharma) that is Hinduism.

The following three suggested activities entwine learning about Hindu values together with learning from these values for your pupils:

- **Good Hindu living. First,** a Hindu children's code for goodness enables children to learn about the moral values of the religion and reflect on their own values through classroom talk.

- **How to be naughty: Secondly,** pupils think about being naughty (and, conversely being good!). This fun activity asks them to create a charter for 'how to be naughty'.

- **Make a play. Finally,** a drama activity asks groups of pupils to explore choices and consequences through improvised plays. This links to the Hindu values and the 'how to be naughty' charter above.

What can children do as a result of this unit?

The following pupil friendly 'I can . . .' statements describe the learning that may be expected of pupils 7–9 years of age.

Level	Description of achievement: I can . . .
1	• **talk about** what is valuable to me. • **talk about** something that matters to Hindu people.
2	• **retell** a simple values story in a drama. • **retell** a simple values story in a drama.. • **respond sensitively** to some Hindu values.
3	• **describe** what Hindu people think is good. • **describe** what I think is good and bad. • **make links** between Hindu ideas and my own ideas.
4	• **use the right words** to show that I **understand** how being a Hindu makes a difference to what people think is good. • **apply** ideas like being harmless, being generous or showing compassion for myself.

An extended version of this material, including a PowerPoint sequence to support learning and a full colour version of 'How to be good' are available for subscribers to download from the RE Today website www.retoday.org.uk; password in this term's issue of the *REtoday* magazine.

How to be good

Always be truthful. Truth is always victorious.

Always be happy. Try to use a smile to help you carry on.

Always face your troubles. Have courage and tolerance.

Do all your work diligently. Be careful, be enthusiastic.

Be humble. Never boast

Be just. Never be unfair to others

Be generous. Not just with money, but with your appreciation of other people.

Don't lose your temper. Try to control your anger.

Accept success or failure at work. Don't be conceited about success, and don't be depressed by failures.

Be polite. You need never be rude to anybody. Never waste words. Always try to speak politely, briefly, with understanding.

Always be compassionate. Never hurt anyone or thing that lives.

Aspire to do difficult tasks. You will attain higher goals in life.

When you eat, thank God. Pray at a meal to be grateful for your food.

Do good deeds. Always.

God is omnipresent. God is everywhere.

You do nothing without God's knowledge

Keep him with you and let him watch over all your life.

About this 'code for good'

This code was published in a magazine for Hindu children and young people in Leicester. The magazine was called *Sanatan Sandesh*.

It gives you 16 ideas about how Hindu religion can show Hindu children good ways to live.

For you to do

- Read this carefully with a partner.
- Highlight **six** ideas from the code which **you agree with most**.
- Highlight **two** that **you don't agree with** in a different colour.

Talk about:

- What can everyone learn from the code?
- Do you have to be Hindu to think the ideas in 'How to be good' are good ideas?
- What would an opposite code, 'How to be naughty', look like?

RE Today
Services

How to be naughty: A cheeky activity

Joe and Daisy have been good children for all their lives, but today they are going to try being naughty for a change. But they don't really know how. Some of you do! Can you help them?

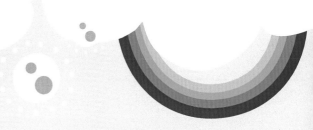

1 Start off by making a list of naughty behaviour in the first column of the table. Then go on to fill in the other columns.

Ten things we think are naughty	Who might be upset if you did this?	A good thing you could do instead of this:
1.		
2.		
3.		
4.		
5.		
6.		
7.		
8.		
9.		
10.		

2 Now look at the two 'charters for being naughty' made by Joanna (9) and Jonathan (8). With a partner: use these charters to work out what Joanna and Jonathan think is GOOD!

3 We can often tell what somebody thinks is good from what they say about being naughty.

● Talk about the charts you have made about good and naughty, and the things you could do instead of being naughty.

● How do your ideas link up to the ideas in the Hindu code for goodness?

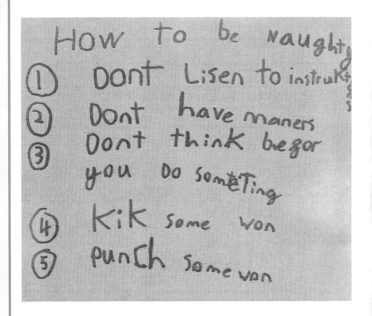

How to be naughty
① Dont Lisen to instruktsges
② Dont have maners
③ Dont think begor you Do someTing
④ Kik some won
⑤ punch some won

Joanna
How to be naughty
① Kick your mums car.
② Hit your dad
③ MESS around in the class
④ Playing around with maches
⑤ swearing at someone
⑥ break a rule
⑦ rip someones work
⑧ steel someons ideas

Consequences drama: six little plays for the whole class

For the teacher

- Put the class into six groups for dramatic improvisation.

- Give out the scenarios from page 23, one per group.

- Ask half of the groups to make a script and develop a drama where there are good consequences, and half to make dramas with dreadful consequences. The idea may need some explanation!

- After pupils have had time to create their improvised plays, watch the dramas two at a time. Between each pair of dramas, look again at the Hindu code for good and the children's codes for being naughty.

- What happened in the dramas that links to the codes?

- Who was following the code for 'how to be good'? Who was living by the 'how to be naughty' codes? Draw attention to the idea that being naughty often makes other people unhappy.

Plenary: What have the children learned: (a) about Hindu ideas about being good? (b) about themselves?

The New Boy

Jodie, Judy and Jade are in the playground. There is a new boy in the school, and the girls decide to play a joke on the new kid. They go up to him and say 'Mrs Jackson wants to see you.'

'Who's Mrs Jackson?' asks Jonathan, the new boy.

'She's the head teacher, silly,' they reply 'She probably wants to tell you off about your sweatshirt. It's not a proper school one, you know. You'd better go and stand by her door.'

Jonathan goes in to the school, and stands by the head teacher's door, looking worried. The girls spy on him, laughing. When playtime is over, they go back to class, still giggling, but Jonathan is still standing by the door . . .

What happens next?

The Changing Room Window

At football on Wednesday after school, Tim, Jim and Kim are messing about in the changing rooms. There is no teacher there.

'I bet you can't climb out of that window,' says Jim to the other two. The window is quite high up, but there is a table to stand on. The boys climb onto the table, and look out of the window, which is open on its hinges. Outside, there is a flat roof. The window is quite big. Tim checks the door. There is no one around.

'You're chickens,' says Jim. 'If you're too scared to do it, I will!'

What happens next?

Breaking the hedge

Sharon, Karen, Darren and Haran are walking home together one day. They go past Mrs Bridge's house, where they usually walk. Yesterday, they had been scrapping on the way home, and fell through the little hedge into her garden. They had broken the flowers there.

Mrs Bridge comes out. 'You children,' she says 'I saw you breaking down my flowers yesterday. Tell me your names. I'm going to phone the school.'

Darren speaks up straight away, but he's not telling the truth: 'No, Miss, it wasn't us. We know the kids who did that, but it wasn't us. You must be mixing us up because we all wear the same school uniform.' He is thinking of four other children. He's going to blame them, give their names, and get out of trouble . . .

What happens next?

LEARNING FROM SIKH VALUES: EQUALITY AND SERVICE

This section enables children to learn about and reflect on the value Sikhs give to being generous and including everyone.

Using a story and the questions that arise from it, and the themes of sharing and service exemplified in the Sikh langar kitchen, these activities will enable children to

- **develop knowledge and understanding** of Sikh beliefs, experiences and practices.

- **reflect on their own beliefs, values, perceptions and experiences** in the light of their learning.

The activities set the foundations for developing **positive attitudes** of respect towards Sikhs and to other people who hold views and beliefs that are different from their own.

Information file

- Every **gurdwara** has a **langar** (kitchen) at which food is served free to all who will eat with everyone else.
  No distinctions of caste, race, colour or age are applied: all share together.

- Sikhs consider it an honour to provide the food served in the langar, and all are welcome. School pupils are often most impressed by this generosity when they visit a gurdwara.

- The gurdwara is the 'house of the Guru' because the presence of the sacred writings in the form of the **Guru Granth Sahib** live there. The text is honoured as a living guru by the community.

What can children do as a result of this unit?

The following pupil friendly 'I can . . .' statements describe the learning that may be expected of pupils 7–9 years of age.

Level	Description of achievement: I can . . .
1	• **name** some Sikh artefacts. (AT1) • **talk about** why Sikhs like to share and why I like to share. (AT2)
2	• **retell** the Sikh story of Dunni Chand and the needle. (AT1) • **identify** a good reason to share. (AT1) • **respond sensitively** to the ideas of being generous, being equal and being fair. (AT2)
3	• **describe** the teaching Sikhs try to follow about sharing equally, making links to the langar. (AT1) • **use religious or spiritual vocabulary** such as gurdwara, sewa, langar, generosity, equality. • **make links** between Sikh ideas about sharing and generosity and my own ideas. (AT2)

Cross-curricular links

These RE activities make a significant contribution to **Spiritual, Moral, Social and Cultural Development of pupils**

Pupil can develop:

- **spiritually** by learning about and reflecting on a story, some artefacts and some values that are at the heart of Sikh practice

- **morally** by considering how religious stories and values lead to particular actions

- **culturally** by encountering people and resources from Sikh ways of life.

The story of Dunni Chand and the needle: what does the story mean?

Guru Nanak was a travelling teacher. He visited Lahore, where there lived a banker called Dunni Chand, well known for being very greedy. His beautiful palace shone with gold, marble and precious jewels.

Dunni Chand learnt that Guru Nanak was visiting. He rushed to invite the Guru to a special feast: it would make him look very important to have such a famous guest!

Guru Nanak accepted the invitation. It was a wonderful occasion. When everyone had finished, Dunni Chand turned to Guru Nanak: 'I am a wealthy man, I can help you. What do you want me to do?' Guru Nanak sat and thought. Fumbling in his pocket, he drew out a tiny sewing needle.

'Something you can do for me,' he replied, holding up the needle. 'I want you to keep this needle very safe and give it back when we meet in the next world.'

Dunni Chand felt very important. The Guru had given him a very special task. He took the needle and showed it to his wife, explaining what the Guru had told him. To his surprise, she burst into laughter. 'How are you going to do that?' she asked.

He thought and thought, then ran back to the Guru asking 'How can I take this needle with me when I die?'

'If you cannot take a tiny needle with you when you die, how are you going to take all your riches?' asked the Guru.

For the first time in his life Dunni Chand felt ashamed. He realised he had been greedy. He and his wife decided to use their wealth to help the poor.

> For an animated telling of this story by Year 6 pupils at Barden Junior School, Lancashire, see www.cleo.net.uk.

W

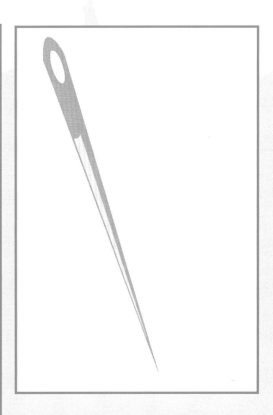

Activities

- Tell the story in an exciting way.

- Ask the pupils in groups to develop a drama about the story. They might make a scene of the story, and then another scene in which Dunni Chand puts his plan into action, and is generous.

- Make lists of all the things the children can think of that show generosity. What could rich Dunni Chand do with his wealth?

- Talk about the idea of the 'next life'. Sikhs believe that when the body dies, there is another life. Thinking about this is what made Dunni Chand change his life.

Why is there a kitchen in a Sikh holy building?
Who is welcome in the kitchen?

Why does a gurdwara need a kitchen?

- Ask pupils what is essential to a holy building. They may know about mosques, churches or mandirs. None of these buildings has to have a kitchen, but every gurdwara needs a langar. Why?

- Download the video on Sikh places of worship from the RE online website http://pow.reonline.org.uk/videos.htm **w** to find out about the 'langar' and how anyone can eat free meals there.

- Use the photograph below (downloadable from the RE Today website for subscribers) to help children answer the question: 'Why do these ladies like helping in the langar?' Talk about the Sikh values that the langar represents.

- Talk about being generous and being treated generously with the pupils. What examples of generous behaviour have they seen in films, or in real life?

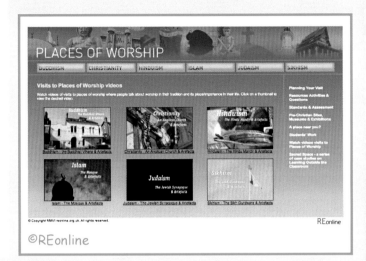

©REonline

©David Rose and NATRE 2009

Hands: a theme for exploring Sikh values and ways of life

For the teacher

- Remind pupils about Sikh values of **sharing** (vand chhakna) and **service** (sewa) to others, represented by the langar. Remind them of the importance of hospitality for Sikhs and how it affects the design of the gurdwara (the langar takes as much space as the prayer hall!)

- Hands feature both in Sikh worship and in service. At the end of worship open hands receive 'prashad', shared by all as a symbol of equality and service. In the langar willing hands prepare and serve the food. Use the following to help children reflect on their own values and attitudes around the themes explored in these activities.

Are we good at sharing and being generous?

- Try this: give two pupils a bag of 'safe in school' sweets. Emphasise that the sweets are theirs to do what they want to with. Ask the rest of the class in groups of five to help one of the group to make a short speech of less than one minute length.

- They must say all the reasons they can think of why their group should have the sweets. Use the prompt 'We should have the sweets because . . .' Listen to the speeches, and then the two with the sweets say what they are going to do.

- Ask the class what advice the Sikh faith would give about the sweets. Talk about why the guru might say that sharing equally is the best thing to do.

- Discuss with the class: What are your values and how do you show what matters to you through how you lead your life?

Receiving hands activity

- Ask children to cup their hands together in a 'receiving' gesture.

- Role play the distribution of prashad in the gurdwara (using sweets or mixed toffees).

- Explain that worshippers in many religions 'receive' food rather than 'take it' as a symbol of receiving God's gifts (such as prashad in the Sikh and Hindu religions, and bread in Christian Holy Communion or Mass).

- Explore the idea of receiving and taking. What do we receive? What do we take? (What is the difference?) Is it better to give than receive? Is it better to receive than to take?

Pupils from Holmer Primary School and Whitecross High School, Hereford, taking part in a Sikh gurdwara role-play activity

Learning from Sikhs: what have we noticed?

At the end of the series of activities, make a table of objects as reminders to pupils. Put out the artefacts, the work done, some sweets, a Lego model of a kitchen for all. Have a 'remembering' conversation:

o What have we learned from the Sikhs?

o What has it made me think about in my own life?

Expressing learning

Give children the outlines from this page to cut out. They then might choose open hands, an outline of the Sikh kara bracelet, an outline of the world or some other image for sharing to help them connect with someone in their own life or experience.

They could:

- draw the most generous person they know (open hands)

- draw a person who is good at remembering God (the Kara)

- draw a person who cares for the planet (world)

and be ready to tell the class about their picture.

RE Today
Services

LEARNING FROM THE BAHÁ'Í FAITH: UNITY

> 'Ye are the leaves of one tree'
> Bahá'u'lláh

For the teacher

This section enables children to learn about and reflect on the value the Bahá'í Faith gives to **unity** – working and living together in harmony.

Using a story and the questions that arise from it, by exploring texts and expressing ideas and responses in reflective and creative activities, children will:

- **develop knowledge and understandin**g of Bahá´í beliefs and values

- **reflect on their own beliefs, values, perceptions and experiences** in the light of their learning.

The activities set the foundations for developing **positive attitudes** of respect towards followers of the Bahá'í Faith and to other people who hold views and beliefs that are different from their own.

Information file

- The Bahá'í Faith is one of the youngest of the world's major religions. It was founded by Bahá'u'lláh in Iran in the nineteenth century.

- Bahá'ís believe in a single God who is known through God's creation and his Messengers.

- Sacred texts: the writings and prayers of Bahá'u'lláh, the Bab, and Abdu'l-Baha are most often used. The Bible, the Qu'ran, and other scriptures are occasionally used in worship.

- Bahá'í religion may be unique in the way that it accepts all other faiths as true and valid. To Bahá'ís, every religion is the religion of God.

- A central idea of the faith is that of **unity**. Bahá'ís believe that people should work together for the common benefit of humanity.

For further background information on the Bahá'í Faith go to the BBC website:

http://www.bbc.co.uk/religion/religions/bahai/index.shtml

Note: Bahá'ís are not allowed to draw any Messengers of God or act their role in a play. This extends to Abdu'l- Bahá, the son of Bahá'u'lláh, as a sign of respect.

What can children do as a result of this unit?

The following pupil friendly 'I can . . .' statements could be used to assess children's responses to the activities. Level 2 describes what most 7-year-olds should be able to do, Level 3 what most 9-year-olds should be able to do.

Level	Description of achievement: I can . . .
1	• **name** one thing which is really important to followers of the Bahá'í Faith. (AT1) • **talk about** why it is good to get on well with others. (AT2)
2	• **retell** the story of The Fingers and say what I think it means. (AT1) • **say what** the message of the story makes me think about for my family, my school, my community. (AT2)
3	• **describe** some metaphors used by Bahá'ís to explain the idea of unity and make up some of my own. (AT1) • **use religious or spiritual vocabulary** such as the Bahá'í Faith, Bahá'u'lláh, and religious beliefs. • **make links** between Bahá'í ideas about unity and my own ideas. (AT2)

Cross-curricular links

These RE activities make a significant contribution to **Spiritual, Moral, Social and Cultural development of pupils**

Pupils can develop:

- **spiritually** by learning about and reflecting on a story and some teachings and values that are at the heart of the Bahá'í Faith.

- **morally** by considering how religious stories and values lead to particular actions.

- **culturally** by encountering people and teachings from the Bahá'í Faith.

Subjects and areas of learning

- Personal development skills, attitudes and attributes

- Art; PSHCE; Literacy.

Story: The Fingers of One Hand

What does the story mean?
How can we explore the story?

Once there was a hand whose fingers had minds of their own. One day the first finger said to himself, 'I think I will play the piano.' So he started hitting the keys on the piano.

The second finger said to himself, 'I think I will draw.' He put a piece of paper on top of the piano. This covered some of the piano keys and made the first finger cross. He was even more cross when the second finger found he could not hold the pencil alone and it fell, hitting the first finger on the nail.

The third finger was feeling rather cold. He decided to put a glove on. He found it very hard to wriggle his way into his own place in the glove. As he tried to get there the glove flapped about. It moved over the piano and the paper. The second finger was cross and the first finger was even more cross.

The little finger had a kind but unwise thought. He had heard the mouth say that it was thirsty. 'I will give him a drink of tea,' said the little finger. He did not think to ask the other fingers for some help. He tried to lift a cup by himself. But he was not strong enough and the tea went all over the place.

The piano was wet, the paper was wet, the pencil was wet and so was the glove!

'STOP!' said the thumb, 'This will never do. We can only do things if we work together. The first finger's tune would sound much better if we all helped him. The second finger needs the rest of us to hold the pencil. It is silly to have just one finger inside a glove. If we are cold we should all wear the glove. And the mouth would have had some tea if we had all helped the little finger.'

From then on they all worked together.

Source: Bahá'í Home Study Programme p.36

Activity 1 Exploring the story

- Tell the story in an exciting way.

- Pair and share ideas about what the story tells us *(that although we are all separate individuals we are all ultimately bound together and need to work together for the good of all)*

- Ask children to suggest ways they could work together to retell this story to others to convey its message.

Expressing meaning

- Children could use creativity to express the ideas in this story. For example they might put card tubes on the fingers of an old glove, each finger illustrating a different person, and the message of the story written on the palm.

Reflecting and applying ideas

- Children could think, talk and write about how living the message of the story would make a difference in their family, school, community and wider world.

Activity 2 Ranking and discussion

How can we have unity in our lives and in the world?

Within the Bahá'í writings are some key principles relating to world unity. They include:

Equality of men and women
Oneness of mankind
Unity of religion
Harmony of science and religion
Elimination of prejudice of all kinds
Universal education
A universal language
Universal peace upheld by a world government

Pupils discuss these principles and then write them on a sheet of paper/card. They cut them out and in small groups rank them according to their potential (i.e. in the children's view) for bringing about world unity. The children give reasons for their choices.

RE Today
Services

What would help us live together as one big family?

How can we achieve unity?

For Bahá'ís the perfect example of a Bahá'í was 'Abdu'l-Bahá, the son of Bahá'u'lláh. All over the world Bahá'ís endeavour to follow his example. This is what he said about how we can live in unity:

> I charge you all that each one of you concentrate all the thoughts of your heart on love and a thought of hatred must be destroyed by a more powerful thought of love.
>
> Thoughts of war bring destruction to all harmony, well-being restfulness and content.
>
> Thoughts of love are constructive of brotherhood, peace, friendship and happiness.
>
> Abdu'l-Bahá, (*Paris Talks*, p.9)

Activity 3   Thoughts of love

In small groups write a list of thoughts that prevent unity in your, classroom, playground or neighbourhood. Next to each one write a thought that could replace each one and result in more unity, e.g. anger/calmness; fear/ courage; revenge/ forgiveness. Share your thoughts with other groups.

Activity 4   Flowers of one garden

Each member of the class makes a large flower from card and paper. In the centre of the flower they place a small photograph of themselves. The flowers should all be different and of many colours just like the human race. They could be placed in a 'garden' on a display board with the quotation about the flowers of one garden from the Bahá'í writings: 'All mankind are the fruits of one tree, the flowers of the same garden, waves of one sea' (Abdu'l-Bahá).

Talk about why garden, tree, sea are good metaphors for the 'unity'. Can children think of others? Make posters to show these.

Activity 5   Create a unity tree

Children make leaves to fix on a twiggy branch. Alternatively the tree could be drawn and painted as in the example below. On their leaves children write their names and a belief, value or attitude, which would help everyone to live together happily and harmoniously.

Talk about which of these would please someone from the Bahá'í Faith.

Ye are the leaves
of one tree
  Bahá'u'lláh

RE SUBJECT LEADER SECTION

Values are principles or fundamental convictions which act as guides to our behaviour.

Beliefs about that which is of fundamental worth lies at the root of these.

RE and values education

Values are principles or fundamental convictions which act as guides to our behaviour. Beliefs about that which is of fundamental worth lies at the root of these. Enabling children to explore beliefs and values in today's world, and to consider and reflect on the practical implications of expressing these in relation to themselves, others, the community and the world is central to religious education.

Many schools take a whole school approach to values development and **RE has a key role to play** in this. RE activities can underpin such approaches by

- helping children **to make the link between what we believe and how we behave.**

- support spiritual and moral development through **reflective exploration** of the wisdom of the faith traditions and in the teaching of key religious figures.

- enabling **children to consider their own beliefs and values and those of others in the light of their learning in religious education.**

What can teachers do?

Many teachers are aware of the great need for children to develop key values such as respect, compassion, hope, peace and love. These spiritual values are shared by the great religions and by those of no religion. Well-planned Religious Education provides lots of opportunities to help children reflect on these values and to think about how they can apply them in their lives.

What kind of school? What kind of teacher?

Questions for reflection for the RE subject leader

- It is widely recognised that a key element of a successful school is the articulation and promotion of **shared values**.
  What are the shared values in your school? How does RE contribute to these?

- Positive values are transmitted when they are **modelled in the day-to-day relationships** in school.
  What values are teachers of RE communicating? e.g. hope, courage, love, wonder – or something less positive? Is RE taught as well as other subjects? If not, why not?

- **Values are transmitted through learning and teaching.**
  Does RE provide children with planned experiences and situations to help them consider and reflect on positive values and engage with the practical implications of expressing these for themselves?

How can I do this?

RE is delivered in such a wide variety of contexts in today's curriculum that subject leaders often ask: *How can I make sure that RE engages children, develops their learning and thinking skills, impacts on their personal development – and meets the requirements of the syllabus?* The RE Today advisory team have produced the process on the next page to outline the key steps to take. Use this to check the RE activities in your school.

RE Today
Services